Revised and Expanded Edition

How I Came to Be a Writer

Phyllis Reynolds Naylor

SCHOLASTIC INC.
New York Toronto London Auckland Sydney
Mexico City New Delhi Hong Kong Buenos Aires

To anyone who ever wanted to write a book,
but especially to my mother, who had enough faith in
me to save my early stories.

The quote on page 67 is from "D.C. Becoming Haven for Teen-Aged Runaways"
by Carl Bernstein from the Washington Post, January 25, 1970.

Acknowledgments appear on page 139, which constitutes
an extension of this copyright page.

ISBN 0-439-47194-X

10   40   11

Foreword

This book will not tell you how to write. It is about my own beginnings—successes and failures, reviews and rejection slips—things that mark the stages in a writer's life.

Every author has his own story. In some ways the stories are different and in some ways they are the same. If you want to write—if you are bursting with things that need putting down on paper—remember that the story of how *you* became a writer has already begun.

1

Starting from Scratch

The idea of being a writer never entered my mind when I was growing up. An occupation, I knew, was something that took years of preparation and hard work, and writing was simply too much fun. So I decided to become a teacher, an actress, an opera singer, a tap dancer, or a missionary.

My mother did not like the thought of my being an actress and told me I would probably faint under the bright lights. She also did not like the idea of my being a tap dancer, so I was never allowed to take lessons. Missionaries, as everyone knew, were sometimes eaten alive, so that left teaching and opera singing. Writing, which was the thing I loved most in the world, was only my hobby.

My parents had always liked books, and they knew a good story when they heard one. My mother, in fact, used to scare her own six brothers and sisters witless with stories she made up, and she was scolded once for telling her younger brother that he was not really one of the family at all, having been found in a ditch by the side of the road. In college, Mother and Dad acted in plays together, and enjoyed the roles of Portia and Shylock in *The Merchant of Venice*. So when we three children came along, we were born into a home that loved stories.

My "coming-out" party took place on January 4, 1933, in Anderson, Indiana. The doctor was attending a theater in Indianapolis that evening, so I surprised my mother by making my appearance all by myself. The last I heard, the little house on Chestnut Street, where I was born, is still there.

When I arrived, the Depression was raging, but the picture of me in my baby book, dressed in hand-me-down clothes and shoes that were much too large, has this caption in my mother's handwriting: "Phyllis Dean, a bright, happy little soul." The truth is, I was too young to mind

Phyllis was born at home in this little house on Chestnut Street, Anderson, Indiana.

being poor. I remember the two checked dresses I wore to kindergarten, one red, the other blue, and Mother telling me that if I alternated colors, it would seem as though I had more clothes than I did. I simply thought how very clever my mother was.

I remember her crying when she broke our fever thermometer, and again when my sister spilled the vanilla, but it didn't particularly concern me. When Mother had to take in the neighbors' laundry in order to help pay our bills, and it was my duty and my sister's to return the finished clothes in a basket, that

Little did anyone know that the first story composed by the angelic child on the right would be about cutting off somebody's head.

This is my mother, father, my big sister, Norma, and me, before my brother, John, was born.

didn't embarrass me either. Norma insisted that we take them back after dark, which I thought ridiculous, since I wasn't afraid of being seen, but I *was* afraid of the dark.

One of the reasons I didn't know we were poor, however, was that we had books. Not many, but we heard them read over and over again—*Egermeier's Bible Story Book,* two volumes of *Grimm's Fairy Tales,* the complete works of Mark Twain, a set of the *Collier's Encyclopedia,* a small collection of Sherlock Holmes books in red covers that the mice had nibbled, and a book with pictures of hell in it—demons cutting people in half and dousing their heads in boiling oil. I don't know what happened to that book, but I was glad when it disappeared.

These were not just books to read, I'm afraid, but they were also our toys. The volumes of the *Collier's Encyclopedia,* stood on end, formed the walls of the first floor of a dollhouse; the Mark Twains became the upstairs; and the Sherlock Holmes books formed the attic. Whenever we stretched bedsheets across the backs of chairs to play train, a good heavy encyclopedia volume held the sheet in place, and books were the tunnels through which my little brother sent his cars spinning. When evening came and it was time for my father to read another chapter from *The Prince and the Pauper,* no one complained that the dollhouse or tunnel had to be dismantled. Even now it bothers me to see, in someone's study, rows of pristine books that look as though they have never been opened, much less read and treasured—and certainly never used for holding a bedsheet in place.

As we grew older, our book collection got bigger, and Mother often brought home books from the library. She read to us every night, almost until we were old enough to go out on dates, though we would never have admitted this to anyone. When my sister considered herself too old to be read to any longer, she would sit at the dining room table doing her homework while Mother read to my brother and me on the couch. She was listening, nonetheless. And when I decided that I was far too sophisticated for books such as *The Little White Bed That Ran Away,* I too would retreat to my arithmetic problems in the dining room. But when I heard those familiar words, "Thump, bumpity, bump, bump; down the stairs came the little white bed," I would sneak over to the couch beside my brother, John, "just to see the pictures." I can

Someone once gave my big sister a large chocolate Easter rabbit and didn't give me anything. So while she was at school one day, I ate the whole thing. We weren't always this loving.

Since these were Depression years, my father bought boys' clothes for me because he thought they would last longer. Here I am in a boy's cap, coat, socks, and shoes. The smile is a fake. I am thinking of murder.

still hear John's shrieks of laughter at the antics of Toad and his motor car in *The Wind in the Willows*—and remember the drama in my mother's voice as she read of the tribulations of the Israelites on their way to the Promised Land.

Our parents often sang to us, too, and many of their songs were really stories: "The Preacher and the Bear," another about a ship going down at sea, and even one about a homeless little girl whose mother was dead. It began:

> *Out in this cold world alone,*
> *Wandering about on the street . . .*

and it ended with a vision of the child's mother looking down on her from heaven. It always made me cry. "Make sombody find the little girl," I frequently begged my mother, and she would add a verse of her own at the end.

Some of the best nights were the ones when my father did the reading. He could imitate all kinds of voices—the runaway Jim's in *Huckleberry Finn*, Injun Joe's in *Tom Sawyer*, and Marley's ghost in *A Christmas Carol*. And when Mother read "Little Orphant Annie" from James Whitcomb Riley's *Child-Rhymes*, ending with "Er the Gobble-uns'll git you/If you Don't Watch Out"

8

(at which point she grabbed us), our hearts pounded. We worshiped those books that had the power to make us shiver. I was never very curious about the authors, though. It was the *story* that was important.

As a small child, I began kindergarten in midyear, since my birthday was in January, and consequently, I was not old enough for first grade when September came. As I watched my friends being escorted, beaming, to the first-grade classroom down the hall, I didn't know why I couldn't go. All I knew was that I had been sitting in the circle a very long time without hearing my name called. Finally, fidgeting about, I put my feet up on an empty chair next to me. The harried teacher, in passing, gave my legs a slap and told me to put them down. For years I believed that I had been kept back because I put my feet on the chair.

That teacher was replaced by another, however, who used to seat herself in the middle of the floor each afternoon and invite us to come to her and "make up a story." She would write down what we said and let us take it home to show to our parents. I remember only one of the stories I composed, but I do remember her telling me to give someone else a chance, that I had had quite enough turns for one day.

My mother, however, saved the first one I brought home, probably in case I should ever need to show it to a psychiatrist:

Once upon a time there was a little boy and a little girl who lived in the woods with their mother. One day the little boy said, "Mother, I want an apple." The mother said, "Okay." The boy reached into the box and the mother closed the lid on him and cut off his head and set him out in the yard and tied a rag around his neck to keep his head on. The little girl came home. She cried a lot. She sneaked out and pasted his head back on with magic paste. Then she put her brother in her boyfriend's house. She grew up and married her boyfriend. The mother died. The end.

This story, I discovered years later, sounds suspiciously like "The Juniper Tree," by the brothers Grimm, so not only was my first writing effort gory, it was plagiarism at that.

I could hardly wait until I could read and write my own books, and when it was finally my turn for first grade, I entered with high expectations. For some reason, however, I couldn't make sense of reading for a time. I would sit with a small group of children while the teacher turned over large sheets of paper tacked onto an easel. Sentences had been written on each page in black crayon, and they seemed to have something to do with the pictures in the right-hand corners—a cat or a dog or a tree in autumn. One by one the other children read aloud those black marks on white paper while I sat mute and unhappy. I can't describe my disappointment. How did the others know, I wondered, that those marks said, "See the dog run?" One day I decided that perhaps reading was just making stories up. So the next time the teacher pointed to the words, I raised my hand and eagerly launched into a story about a vicious dog attacking a cat beneath a tree in autumn. The teacher looked at me sadly and shook her head, and I knew that I still had not discovered the magic secret.

I don't know just when it was that reading "clicked" with me, but once I learned, I could not get enough of it. The advanced reading books always seemed to have the most exciting stories, and how I wanted the class to hurry through one so we could get to the others before the year was out! So many stories, so many books, and so little time to read them all.

By the time I reached third grade, reading

was my favorite subject. In my school, the library consisted of a truck that came around every few weeks. The driver would carry in box after box of books and line them up on the window ledges in the school corridor. Then, one class at a time, we went out into the hall and chose some. I was disappointed when our class was the last to go, because there were so few good books left.

Like many children who love to write, I wrote poems for all occasions. And like most parents, mine tucked these little verses away in the keepsake trunk. There are certain words and phrases that bring smiles of approval from grown-ups, words such as love, sunlight, flowers, church, and prayer. These words are real winners. That's why I was complimented on the following poem, composed on a visit to my paternal grandparents' home when I was nine:

THIS FARM IN MARYLAND

I love this farm in Maryland,
It's full of fun and cheer,
There is one thing that makes it so:
The people living here.

I love the garden growing here,
The sunlight is so bright,
I love the sound of toads and birds,
Chirping in the night.

I love the flowers growing here,
Red, green, and blue,
And all the pretty rocks and birds,
Full of different hues.

I love the little pond here,
With lilies resting there,
And pine trees all around it,
Refreshed with summer air.

I love the church and the pastor,
And the people attending there,
I love our little services,
Full of praise and song and prayer.

This state is very colorful,
Green trees against red sand,
O, if I could but stay here.
This place in Maryland.

I dedicated it, of course, to my grand
(my grandfather himself w

grandparents, naturally, thought it splendid.

Not all of my early poems and stories were so sweet and sentimental, however. Here is another:

> *I know a bad boy,*
> *That will not mind his mother,*
> *But when he is very bad,*
> *He kicks his baby brother.*

I began to be "on call" as an impromptu writer. In fifth grade, the teachers suddenly decided to throw a surprise party for the principal, and I was asked if I would mind staying in during recess to compose a birthday poem. I could write one in twenty minutes, couldn't I? Twenty minutes and one stomachache later, I had produced eight lines that were read over the microphone in the assembly room.

now writing little books of my own.

ld rush home from school to see

ld any discarded paper that

not allowed to use

and drawing,

r. I would

times

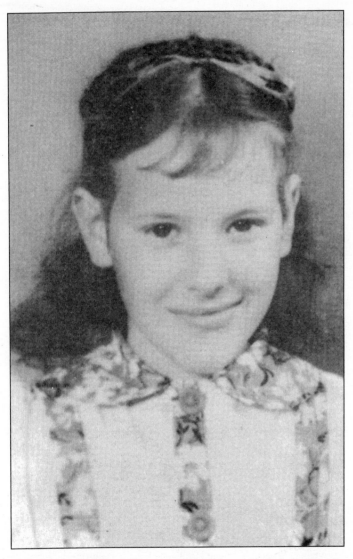

By the time I was ten, my favorite hobby was writing little books. My spelling was, and still is, unremarkable.

give it the appearance of a bound book. Then I would grandly begin my story, writing the words at the top of each page and drawing an accompanying picture at the bottom. Sometimes I typed the story before stapling the pages. Occasionally I even cut an old envelope in half and pasted this on the inside cover as a pocket, slipping an index card inside it, like a library book, so I could check it out to friends and neighbors. I was the author, illustrator, printer, binder, and librarian, all in one.

I wrote about witches and little Dutch boys and animated fire engines. I wrote a series of mystery books about a gorgeous girl named Penny who was always being rescued by her boyfriend, and, because I had just learned to draw lace, somewhere in every "Penny" book, my heroine lost her clothes just so I could draw her lacy underwear. I wrote of elves and fairies and talking refrigerators, and when my mother explained the facts of life to me, I even wrote a book called *Manual for Pregnant Women,* with illustrations by the author. I don't know what happened to that book, but once I showed it to my mother, I never saw it again.

But I never considered myself "bookish." There seemed to be something decidedly

The Food Fairies, Book 1.

unhealthy about people who sat around in garrets fiddling with words instead of going out and living life in the flesh. I liked to make all kinds of things, not just books. I enjoyed having a finished product when I was through, whether it was a pot holder, a wagon, a house made of clay, or a poem. Summers were spent snitching ice off the back of the ice truck, sliding down a grassy hill on pieces of cardboard, building a clubhouse out of old coffin crates, and creating our own Tarzan movies by leaping off fences and walls. Reading was reserved for bedtime.

When I reached junior high school, I enjoyed writing stories more than ever, but friends were important, too. Sometimes in the evenings, when I heard them calling out to me from the porch, I'd be torn between wanting to stay in my room and write and wanting to be with them. That was why I liked rainy nights and snowy weekends, when I knew that no one would be going out and I could write undisturbed.

When I was a freshman in high school, I first experienced a classroom response to my writing. Our assignment was to write something original, either a poem or a story, and read it aloud.

Because it was December, I wrote a poem called
"Christmas Shopping":

It is now one week before Christmas;
I started my shopping last night;
I left as a young stylish woman,
And returned home looking a fright.
I'd put on my warmest clothing,
And after the kids had been kissed,
I frantically ran to the corner
To wait for the bus I'd just missed.
The doorways in town were all crowded
With thousands of women and men,
So, using my elbows as weapons,
I charged through the mob and fell in.
I saw what I wanted at counter four,
And waited, oh, so patiently!
But when the clerk asked, "Who is next, please?"
The lady behind shouted, "Me!"
I gave her my most ferocious look
To show I was horribly mad,
But sunk to my knees when I finally learned
That this shopper bought all that they had.
I had been in town for five hours,
And all of my presents were wrapped,
But in fighting my way to the exit,
My garter suddenly snapped.

I limped on out to the sidewalk.
No one would see it out there—
My nose was running right down to my chin
And the wind blew the pins from my hair.
The bus was just rounding the corner,
The whole town was there to get on.
And in plowing my way to the center
I discovered my strength almost gone.
I smiled a sweet, "That's quite all right,"
To an ox who just flattened my toe,
And stopped to dig out a baby
I had trampled head down in the snow.
I felt the warmth from the bus door
And my tiredness started to ease,
But as I lifted one foot to get on,
The driver called out, "Next bus, please."
I staggered back to the sidewalk,
And solemnly wiped back a tear,
And I prayed as I leaned 'gainst the storefront,
Thank God, this just comes once a year!

When I read the poem, bursts of laughter drowned me out, and I had to wait to be heard. Even the teacher was laughing. But my joy was short-lived, because she called me up to her desk afterward and said, "Phyllis, are you quite sure you didn't copy that poem from a magazine?" It was certainly worth an A, she told me, but she was adding a minus in case I really hadn't written it myself. Perhaps I should have taken this as a compliment, but I was hurt that she didn't trust me.

I spent my time writing skits for my youth group at church, poems for birthdays and anniversaries, and funny letters to fond relatives, with no idea that my first published story was just around the corner

2

A Bubble Bursts

When I was sixteen, a former Sunday School teacher, Arlene Stevens Hall, wrote to me. She said that she was now the editor of a church school paper, that she remembered how much I liked stories, and wondered if I would care to write one for her.

I was delighted and began thinking about what my story would be. I remembered reading something in the newspaper about a baseball player who lost some fingers on his right hand, and this gave me the idea for "Mike's Hero." I typed it up and sent it off:

MIKE'S HERO
by Phyllis Reynolds

"That's all for today, boys," called Mr. Evans as he climbed off the bleachers and walked over to the boys. "If you play that well for our tournament, we'll win for sure."

The boys picked up their bats and crowded around their coach. "Do you really think so?" asked Mike, as he pushed back his red hair.

"Sure we will," answered Jack, who played second base. "We've got the best cub scout baseball team in Galesburg. Don't you think so, Mr. Evans?"

The coach smiled as he looked down at his team. "We'll see who's really the best when we play the big game. Now you had better hurry home. We practiced a half-hour overtime this afternoon. Remember, Wednesday afternoon for our next practice. I'll see you then."

"Okay, Coach," shouted the boys. "Good-bye."

Mike brushed the dirt from his uniform and waited for Ted.

"Whew!" said the dark-haired boy as he walked up to Mike. "That really was a workout! I'm hungry as a bear."

"So am I," said Mike. "Mother said she was going to bake some raisin cookies. Stop in a minute and I'll give you a handful."

The thought of raisin cookies made the boys hurry. As they neared the busy corner of Barton and Jackson streets, the boys' happy expressions changed. Little two-year-old Patty, sister of one of the baseball players on the opposite team, was running toward the street. Ted yelled and Mike started running. Ted followed. Patty ran into the street just as a car swung around the corner. Mike dashed in front of the car, pushing Patty to safety, but the auto hit Mike. There were screams and cries, slamming of brakes, the shouting of directions, and Mike was rushed to the hospital.

The red-haired boy lay unconscious for hours. At times he mumbled a few words about baseball or let out a frightened cry to Patty. It was a week before visitors were allowed to see him. Then Mother and Dad came every day, of course, and Patty's mother came thanking Mike again and again for saving Patty's life. Many others came too: Rev. John Martin, the minister; the driver of the auto, whose name was Mr. Murphy; and even the coach and the team.

Mike would not be able to play baseball for a long time. He had injured the nerves in his right hand. It would be some time before he could again use it well.

Mike did not say much to anyone. He tried to smile and joke with the gang. The team sent him candy, books, and even a portable radio so he could listen to ball games. Mr. Martin came frequently to sit by his bed and talk to him. Mr. Murphy came often. Coach Evans and the team came once a week.

Mike had had his heart set on playing with a big league someday. His baseball hero was Dick Burnhart, who played in one of America's biggest leagues. Now Mike's dreams of becoming a second Burnhart were ruined.

My first story was published when I was sixteen. It was written without effort, with scarcely any revision at all. I wouldn't even have to work for a living! What a life!

The illustration for "Mike's Hero" that appeared with the story in *Boy's and Girl's Comrade.*

Tuesday came, the day of the cub scout tournament. Ted had promised to come to the hospital right after the game and tell Mike which team had won. Mike lay on his back, watching the ceiling. He wished Ted would come.

He heard the nurse in the hall and sat up. Ted came into the room. "Did we win?" asked Mike anxiously.

Ted smiled and laid down his cap. He shook his head. "Nope. They were better than we thought. It was pretty close, though," he added cheerfully.

Mike lay back on his pillow.

"That's too bad," he said sadly.

"Gee, Mike, don't feel bad. You know that we could have won if you had been there. We'll play them again next year and you'll be able to catch for us."

Weeks later Mike was taken home from the hospital. He was thin and white. School had begun but Mike was not able to go.

"He needs a long rest," the doctor said. "He would get along better if he were not so unhappy. I wish I could think of something to cheer him up."

One morning Mike's mother came into his bedroom and woke him up. "I have a surprise for you, Son," she said. "Let me help you wash your face and comb your hair. Then you will have some visitors."

"Who are they, Mom?" he coaxed. "Please tell me."

But Mother just smiled. When Mike was ready, Mother

left the room and returned with four men. First came Coach Evans, then Mr. Murphy and Mr. Martin, and then—no, it couldn't be, but it was—Dick Burnhart, Mike's baseball star!

Mike's eyes shone and he sat up quickly. "Dick Burnhart," he cried. "I never thought I'd meet you!"

"I never thought I would meet you either, Mike. I don't get a chance to meet heroes every day." Dick sat down on the edge of the bed.

"Heroes," exclaimed Mike. "You're the hero, Mr. Burnhart."

"No," said the famous man. "I'm just a ballplayer with lots of luck and practice. You're the hero. You saved a little girl's life. That's why I came to see you. Mr. Evans told me all about you. I'm proud of you."

"Proud of me?" asked Mike in surprise.

"Sure," Dick said. "Besides, you're going to take my place someday, and I decided I'd better meet you."

Mike's eyes fell. "But my hand," he said. "How can I take your place?"

Dick held out his own right hand. "Look," he said.

"Why, there are three fingers missing. How do you play ball?"

"I lost my fingers while I was working on a machine, Mike. I thought I could never play ball again. But I wanted to very badly, so I practiced and practiced and kept trying. Sometimes I played poorly and other times I played well. But

I kept trying and practicing until I got on the big league team."

"Gee, Mr. Burnhart, that's swell! Do you suppose I could learn? I'll really try."

"Sure, Mike. Anyone can succeed if he tries hard enough and long enough. As soon as you are able to go outside, start praticing again. I brought you my catcher's mitt. You can keep it." Dick rose and started toward the door. *"Good-bye now, Mike. Hurry and get well soon."*

Mike hugged the catcher's mitt happily. "You bet I'll be well, Dick," he said firmly. *"I'm going to take your place someday."*

It's embarrassing now to read this story. There are too many things wrong with it to list them all, but it's too sentimental, for one. The characters don't talk like real people, for another. And it's not only quite a coincidence that Mike hurt the same hand as his baseball idol, but implausible that, having worshiped Dick Burnhart for so long, Mike didn't know that the man had three fingers missing.

Still, the story was the best that I could do at the time, and it was written expressly for the Sunday School market. Because church school papers paid so little, they were always looking for material, and a few weeks later, I received a check for $4.67. I was thrilled. Imagine being paid for something that was so much fun! Where was the work? Where was the struggle? The words came effortlessly, and I simply wrote them down! What a life!

Send me more, my teacher-turned-editor said. So I wrote all kinds of stories and poems and sent them off: poems for Halloween, Thanksgiving, and Christmas; adventure stories of dramatic rescue; tales of contests won and contests lost; and epics about unkind children who saw the error of their ways. Most of these stories were accepted, and when editing was needed, my kind teacher did it herself. Her criticisms were always gentle and accompanied by encouraging words.

Why, I began to wonder, should I waste my talent on a church school paper when there were dozens of beautiful slick magazines out there just calling me? Why not write for *Children's Playmate, Jack and Jill, Highlights for Children, Boys' Life,* and *Seventeen?*

I spent hours writing up stories with cute titles bound to win an editor's heart: "Mrs. Wiggins' Walrus," "Willie, the Window Glass," "Snipper McSnean and His Flying Machine," "Danny the Drainpipe," and "Miranda, the

Musical Mouse." Then I wrote another batch of exotic stories for teenagers: "The Cobra and Carol," "The Silent Treatment," "The Red Comb," and "Destination, Trouble." I typed them neatly and sent them off with stamped, self-addressed return envelopes to magazines all over the country. Then I sat back and waited for the money to roll in.

The first thing I discovered was that unknown editors did not reply as promptly as my loving former teacher. Weeks went by, sometimes months, before I began to hear from any of them.

The second thing I discovered was that the stories came back with printed rejection slips, not page-long letters of apology with encouragement to try again.

And the third thing I discovered was that all those big, beautiful magazines had been calling to someone else, not to me, because every story winged its way home. For two whole years I sent out stories, and for two years every single one of them came back.

I decided that I had the sort of talent only a Sunday School teacher could love. How the editors must have laughed at my stories! They had probably shown them around the office as examples of just how dreadful stories could be. I was determined to end my short writing career before it got any worse. I wrote to all the editors who were still holding manuscripts of mine and asked that they be returned immediately. I was going burn them. Never again would I humiliate myself in this way.

All the manuscripts but one came back, and in its place came a check for sixty dollars. It was for a story called "The Mystery of the Old Stone Well," and it wasn't even a particularly good story.

I was amazed. From the time I had sent it out until I heard from the editor, I'd thought of all kinds of things in it that needed changing. But if I could get sixty dollars for a story, why not try again—with the very best stories I could write? I did, and five months later, I sold a story to still another editor who had never heard of me before.

My dreams of fame and fortune had vanished along with all the money I had spent on stamps and envelopes over the past two years; they were replaced with a new respect for the business of writing. I merely had one toe in the door, I knew, and had not even begun to climb the stairs.

3

The Long Climb

Slowly, with many rejection slips along the way, I began selling stories to still more church school papers. Some editors were very sympathetic and helpful. They wrote little notes on the printed rejection forms, telling me specifically what it was that made them return my story. Others plainly considered me a curse, I'm sure of it. They returned my manuscript only days after I'd mailed it, with nothing more than a piece of paper on which was printed the single word "Sorry."

Here is a sample of correspondence from one editor who never bought a single story of mine:

First Letter:
As I see it, you haven't caught on how to write stories.

Here you have a fine lad, drifting with the stream, and someone comes along and pulls him to shore. He doesn't even have to stroke. That doesn't make a story, and I want a story, not an incident or a simple piece of well-done narrative.

Second Letter:

Always glad to hear from you. Send manuscripts any time. But I'll never buy any unless you learn the basics of a story. There must be a problem and the main character must struggle with the problem and solve it—not some rich uncle, a good pal like the girl here, not an act of God, not a coincidence, not a fond mother, not an anonymous letter, etc., etc.

Third Letter:

Well, I've read a lot of your stories—writings, I should say, because they aren't stories. Really, I hate to see you waste so much energy on writings that miss the point.

On the other hand, here is the kind of acceptance note that cheered me on:

Dear Phyllis,

Regarding One Small Part of Living: Excellent! I love you. More, please!

My writings were still not very original. The plots were predictable. Mothers were always soft-spoken and understanding, fathers were always fair, grandparents were kindly people who sat about with shawls over their shoulders, and children were always getting into trouble, and sorry about it when it was over.

I had started out with adventure stories for the nine-to-twelve set, and soon decided I wanted to write for the teenage market as well. I wrote about slum life and floods and romances gone awry, and an editor suggested very kindly that I might like to choose one age group and stick with it. "Most writers do that," she said. It was my first sad indication that whatever the really professional writers did, I didn't.

I felt most in touch with myself, however, when I took on the viewpoints of different characters. It was a way of combining past, present, and future, of hanging onto the child I was at seven, yet practicing what I would be like at seventy. This was one area where I disagreed with an editor; I went on eventually to write for adults as well as preschoolers.

When I was a senior in high school, I was appointed Senior Class Poet, probably because no one else wanted the honor. My job was to write a poem for the traditional Ivy Day ceremony preceding graduation. It was a mediocre poem, I know now—"The ivy grows; it climbs ever upward, higher and higher"—that sort of thing. Fortunately I didn't know how bad the poem was then, which enabled me to stand before the five-hundred members of our senior class and recite it.

I married when I was eighteen, and enrolled in the local junior college. After graduation, I moved to Chicago with my husband, where he continued work on his Ph.D. I was employed for several years as a clinical secretary in the university hospital. Then, because I had passed a state examination, I worked for six months as a third-grade teacher.

My husband suggested books I might like to read, and my private education began with Thackeray's *Vanity Fair*, followed by several books by Dickens. There was *War and Peace* and the plays of Shakespeare, the collected works of Sigmund Freud, and *The Canterbury Tales* by Chaucer. We would read to each other from Balzac, Samuel Butler, or George Santayana.

For several months I put myself on a steady diet of nineteenth-century novels by Dostoevski, Flaubert, Tolstoy, and Zola. Then I read more modern books by Sinclair Lewis, Upton Sinclair, John Steinbeck, and William Faulkner. Because these weren't school assignments, I could fling myself into the books, not having to

Appointed Senior Class Poet, Phyllis had to compose a poem and recite it at the Ivy Day ceremony. Joliet (Illinois) Township High School, 1951

worry about outlines or underlining the major themes. I could even read the last chapter first, if I wanted. But always, when I wasn't working or reading, I wrote.

My writing was so far from sounding like Tolstoy or Faulkner that it's a wonder I continued to write at all. But I began to glimpse the possibilities in writing the unexpected. What if a mother was *not* soft-spoken, and a father was *not* fair? Why should children always be the ones at fault? What if grandfathers had something on their minds besides warm weather and woolens?

FOR THOSE WHO THINK YOUNG

Back in 1920, Grandpa Grinager was known as the cat's pajamas. Today he might have been called a swinger, except that he was sixty-nine, not sixteen, and had arthritis of the knees or something.

He was far from senile. Every morning he did his exercises—

no deep-knee bends, to be sure, but he performed a few calisthenics and managed a push-up or two if the weather was dry. Then he went downstairs and fried an egg, the only thing he'd learned to cook since Grandma Grinager died, and usually finished off breakfast with store-bought pie.

After that his day consisted of going down to the drugstore, admiring the pretty girls, listening to a ball game, or doing a bit of gardening. Then he'd change clothes and go down to the Chinese-American restaurant for supper or go over to Fifth Street for spaghetti. And finally, he'd round up the evening with a good detective story.

This, however, was all BJR—Before Jim and Rita—ages sixteen and thirteen respectively. Meg, Gramp's daughter, persuaded him to move in with her and Ralph and the children, and it had seemed like a good idea.

And so he came from Connecticut to Baltimore and was installed in a little room all his own near the front, "where he could watch the cars go by," as Meg put it. And that's about all he did. The family accepted him as one accepts a thirteenth-century lamp and treated him accordingly.

"Good grief, Gramps," said Rita when she found him walking around the house in his bare feet. "You want to get pneumonia of the liver or something?" And after hearing this five or six times, Grandpa Grinager decided maybe there was a pain down there somewhere; so he put on the wool slipper-socks Rita had made him for Christmas.

"C'mon, Gramps, let's go for a drive," young Jim would say, taking his grandfather's elbow as he ushered him down to the car. Then they'd drive out in the country to see all the peaceful brown cows eating peaceful green grass, and Grandpa Grinager would wonder what people in Baltimore did for excitement, anyway. He'd end up falling asleep and Jim would figure it had been too much for him. So the next time they'd skip the cows and concentrate on cornfields, which Gramps hoped never to see again as long as he lived.

Sometimes the family would take Gramps to dinner. They passed up the pizza parlors and the chop suey joints and the shish kebab places and took him to a dreary little place called Mrs. Ritter's Kitchen, where the most exciting thing on the menu was meat loaf. They worried about his digestion and even had him wondering if lemon meringue and sauerkraut were too much for a man his age.

At church on Sunday morning, Gramps would stand outside with Rita before the service, and all her friends would ask if he thought it would rain. Grandpa Grinager didn't know, didn't care, and began to wonder if the younger generation mistook him for a barometer.

And just when he'd been waiting all week to watch the Miss America pageant on television, he discovered that the young people were monopolizing the TV that night and had thoughtfully bought him a book of crossword puzzles.

"Creepers, Kathy, he's practically seventy!" Rita said to

39

her girlfriend. "He needs his rest! Turn the TV down!"

And so Gramps, enjoying the strains of the combo that came drifting into his bedroom, heard the music cut short and promptly fell asleep out of sheer boredom.

Something, he decided, had to be done. He could practically feel himself shriveling up, from his ankles to his elbows, and bones that had never hurt before were hurting now. He was even getting pains in his false teeth.

Obviously, he had to change his image. He could always buy a green felt hat and a yellow vest. He could take karate lessons or join a scuba class at the Y. He could even elope with the church secretary and create the biggest scandal since the minister's cat gave birth in the belfry. But as it turned out, nothing quite so drastic was needed.

It was a fine Saturday morning. When Gramps got out of bed, he decided it would be a lot more fun to do push-ups in his underwear than in his clothes; so he pulled down the blinds and did his calisthenics. Afterward, he sat down in the rocking chair to decide whether to walk over to the park or the courthouse, and covered himself with a quilt while he thought about it. He'd just decided to go to the Pancake House, instead, for a stack of strawberry pancakes when Rita tapped on the door and stuck her head inside.

"Your oatmeal's ready, Gramps," she called.

"Don't think I want any this morning, Rita," he said, wondering if he should tell her about the strawberry pancakes.

But Rita was gone; so he closed his eyes again and wondered if maybe blueberry wouldn't taste better. Or pecan or peanut butter.

Rita, meanwhile, dashed into the kitchen, her eyes wide. "Mother," she cried, "he's sitting there in his chair with a blanket around him and the shades drawn and he doesn't want to eat!"

The next thing Gramps knew, the family was gathered outside his door and he heard Meg's husband say, "What's the matter with him? You sure he's breathing?"

"He won't eat or anything!" Rita exclaimed. "He won't even look out the window."

They all peeped in. Gramps didn't move. He even tried holding his breath and counting to fifteen. And when he got to twelve, he had a most wonderful idea. He almost chuckled out loud.

"Gramps," said Meg, "wouldn't you like to go out for a little air this morning?"

Gramps tried not to laugh as he made his voice waver. "No, Meg. I think I'll just sit here in my chair today."

"No oatmeal, Gramps? Can I bring you a tray?"

"No, I'm not hungry . . . nothing at all," Grandpa Grinager replied, wondering if they could hear his stomach rumbling beneath the blanket. Pineapple. Pineapple pancakes. That would have been perfect.

What happened next was exactly what he predicted. The doctor arrived. Gramps fully intended to let him in on his

The illustration that accompanied "For Those Who Think Young."

little joke, but Meg hovered around the door, so he couldn't.

"He's fit as a fiddle, physically," he heard the doctor tell her in the hall. "Sometimes it's just plain senility and they're better off in a nursing home. But if I were you, I'd try to snap him out of it. The trouble with Gramps is he thinks he's too old to have any fun in life. (Gramps almost choked laughing.) You've got to convince him he's well and strong. Get him interested in bright, lively things. Persuade him to go to new places, see new things. It's worth a try."

Good ole Doc, Gramps thought, settling back in his chair and wiggling his toes in anticipation. *This is going to be fun.*

At eleven o'clock, Jim bounded in. "C'mon, Gramps, let's go for a drive."

"You go on alone, Jim," said Gramps. "I'm feeling sort of weak."

"Oh, no," said Jim. "C'mon. It'll do you good." He pulled off the blanket and handed Gramps a red plaid shirt. "Put it on—nice to have a change," he said, and Gramps obeyed.

The cat's pajamas, he thought as he admired himself in the mirror. But aloud he said, "You sure it looks OK, Jim—for a man my age?"

"You look great, Gramps! A real swinger! Let's go."

"How about a ride out in the country?" said Jim, rolling down the car window.

Cows, thought Gramps. *Stupid, peaceful cows—chewing, chewing, chewing. . . .*

"That will be fine, Jim," he said, leaning back and closing his eyes. "So quiet, so peaceful. . . ."

Jim swung the car around. "Changed my mind, Gramps," he said. "Gonna take you down to the dock section and watch the boats unload."

Now you're talking, Gramps thought, his eyes open again, and he felt like taking the wheel himself to get there faster.

Afterward, they were both starved, and Jim was heading over toward Mrs. Ritter's Kitchen when he suddenly veered off to the left.

"Gramps, you ever eat pizza?" he asked.

Should I lie? Gramps wondered. Or should he confess to putting away several dozen mushroom and anchovy creations in the last two years?

"Pizza?" said Grandpa Grinager. "Must be Italian, huh?"

"The best," said Jim. "Absolutely the best."

This time Gramps could not contain himself. Jim stared as he devoured it all. He could scarcely wait to get home and tell the others.

"Why, Ma, he's like a new man!" Gramps heard him say in the kitchen. "He forgot all about his arthritis and his liver!"

Rita took over next. She rearranged his room, persuaded him to grow a neat little beard, and bought him a dart board.

Then Meg got him to join a bowling team, and Ralph bought him a yellow plaid vest.

Grandpa Grinager let them have their way. He accompanied Jim to Saturday afternoon football practice, and Rita to the park for sketching. He was constantly exhorted to wear bright colors, read the latest books, and visit new places. He balked only once and that was when they tried to set up a date between him and the church secretary. But he was having the time of his life.

"You've no idea what we've done for him!" he overheard Rita telling her girlfriend over the phone. "Why, he was moping around as though he were ninety-seven or something, and you should see him now!"

"Just had to be convinced he wasn't old," Jim was heard to say from the front porch. "A man will just go to pot if you let him sit around thinking about his aches all day. Teach him to think young! That's all he needed!"

And Grandpa Grinager, sitting inside with a detective book and a bag of pretzels, smiled, buttoned his yellow plaid vest, and decided to walk down the street for a double malted.

At long last, I could see some change in my writing. When I read my earlier stories, I was able to spot predictable endings and stilted dialogue. I realized that style, whatever it was, was developing without my thinking too much about it.

"I knew this was your story as soon as I read

the opening line," one editor wrote to me, and I wondered how she knew.

In my early years of writing, I usually wrote everything over, from beginning to end, about three times before I felt that it was good enough to send in. That seemed an enormous amount of work to me then, and I'm glad I didn't know that someday I would find myself agonizing several days over a single paragraph. The first draft of a story was always the most difficult, because I was building the basic framework. Once that was down on the paper, the revisions seemed to come easier.

I never showed my stories to anyone other than editors before they were published, because it wasn't until they were accepted that I was sure the stories were any good. Somehow it seemed easier sending them off to a distant editor to accept or reject than to risk having someone close to me laugh at them.

Now the search was on for ideas.

4

The Things That Make Up Me

A poet—a real, published poet—lived next door to us when I was a teenager, and she gave me her old copies of *The Writer* magazine. I don't remember too much more about her, except that she told me never to give up. What I do remember is the number of articles in *The Writer* that said you should write about what you know best.

I didn't know very much. The farthest I had ever been was Louisiana, and the only unusual things that had ever happened to me were: (1) I almost got hit by a train when I was five, and (2) I almost drowned when I was six. Since nobody saw me run across the tracks except the engineer, and nobody realized I was drowning except the cousin who rescued me, nobody made much of a fuss, so these incidents didn't seem like stories. In my later writing, I would use the feelings I'd had at the time, but in my early search for ideas, these did not seem good possibilities at all.

What had influenced me, I knew, was a youth fellowship group in the church I attended as a teenager. My close friends were from this group, and most of our social life revolved around church activities. Why not concentrate on that?

At the same time, however, I wanted my writing to be different. I felt that many of the stories in church magazines, including some of my own, had characters in them that were just too good to be true. They certainly never seemed to think the same thoughts that I did. And why were the stories always so serious?

I decided to try a humor column for teenagers, which I'd write from the viewpoint of a fifteen-year-old boy. (I was afraid that if I wrote it from a girl's point of view, boys would never read it.) I took the pseudonym P. R. Tedesco and called the series "First Person Singular." I wanted to focus on P. R. Tedesco's relationships with his teachers, his friends, and his parents, and make the whole series sort of zany.

In the beginning, only one editor was interested. "I like them," she said, "but can I count on you to write a column every week, fifty-two columns a year?"

She could. The column lasted twenty-five years and appeared under various titles in a number of church magazines across the country. Readers wrote that they always looked forward to finding the column on the last page of their church school paper. Here is a sample, called "Go-Between":

My folks don't quarrel very often, but when they do I feel all insecure inside. I mean, my throat tightens up and my pupils dilate and I get palpitations of the liver or something.

So this afternoon when I went out in the kitchen for a bologna sandwich and found my parents quarreling, I sort of slunk in sideways and wished I could do something to restore peace and tranquillity.

Mom was practically screaming. "All weekend," she cried, "you've been absolutely unbearable! No matter what I say, you disagree with me!"

"So what do you want!" Dad croaked. "A doormat? Of all the ridiculous suggestions! Whoever heard of a back porch floor made of concrete, marbles, and bottle caps!"

"Yeah, Ma," I said, trying to be mediator. "The bottle caps gotta go. That's pretty dumb."

"So who asked you?" cried Mother. "If the Decorator's Guide can take five hundred Coke bottle caps and—"

"And who's going to drink the five hundred Cokes?" roared Dad. "Of all the idiotic ideas, this is—"

"Oh, I don't know now, Pop," I said, reaching for the bologna. "It sort of grabs me after all, now that I think about it. I drink ten Cokes a day for fifty days, and you have all the caps you need."

"Ten Cokes a day!" said Mother. "I should say not!"

"What do you think this is?" Dad boomed. "A mint?"

"Anything for the cause," I said. "'Course, if you're willing to wait I could cut it down to five a day for one hundred days."

"You're out of your mind," said Mother. "Bottle caps are out."

"Plain concrete is much more practical," said Dad.

"Absolutely," said Mom.

So I took my bologna sandwich and ambled on up to my room, wondering how much I should charge when I get to be a marriage counselor.

Because I could write about anything at all in the column—friends, fears, parents, school, God—ideas were not hard to think up. By the time I discontinued the series, I had learned to write about serious subjects—segregation, prejudice, capital punishment, and the Vietnam War—in a sardonic way that would still interest teenage readers. The most difficult problem, strangely, was answering an occasional fan letter like this one:

Dear Mr. Tedesco:
You really tell it like it is, Man! What does your girlfriend think of your writing?

"But how do the ideas keep coming?" people asked.

I once asked an artist that same question. A simple walk down the street, she told me, gave her a dozen ideas—the pattern of light on a wall, the texture of somebody's stockings, the tangle of branches against the sky. . . .

That was the way it was with me. After a while, one idea led to another, and I began to see possibilities in all sorts of things that earlier I would have dismissed as not worth writing about. It was not so much *what* I wrote about, I discovered, as *how* I wrote about it. After all, almost anything that could ever happen to a human being had already been written about, by someone, somewhere. The difference would be in the treatment, the style.

Sometimes ideas came easily, handed to me in the daily newspaper. I once read about a dog that lived with one family for a number of years, then ran away and was taken in by a second family for five years after that. One day, of course, the first owner saw the dog being walked by the second, and there was a lawsuit. So I wrote a story for *Jack and Jill* about a dog that lived with one family during the day and then, at night when they let him out, went to live with a second family.

Another time I read about a crowd that gathered outside a church where a man was threatening to jump from the steeple. At first the crowd was fearful, but as the man delayed, the spectators became impatient and taunted him to jump. The article bothered me so much that I wrote a story about just such an incident, trying to work out in my own mind what it was that would make people behave in this way. At the end of my story, the man jumped. Some editors objected and felt he should have been rescued. So many other editors *did* like the story, however, that it was reprinted again and again.

There were other times that ideas did not come quite so easily. I found it helpful then to just sit down in a quiet place and get reacquainted with myself. What things were important to me? What did I know so well I could almost write about it with my eyes closed?

Singing was very important to me, even though—alas—I was never good enough to become an opera star. So I combined singing and humor to write about something I did not like at all, unfamiliar church hymns:

ALL SIX VERSES, YET!
In unison we rise and stand
And wish that we were sitting.
We listen to the music start,
And wish that it were quitting.
We pass our hymnal to a guest
or fake a smoker's cough;
We drop our pencils, lose our gloves,
Or take our glasses off.
We move our lips to keep in style,
Emitting awkward bleats,
And when the last "Amen" is sung,
Sink gladly in our seats.
O Lord, who hearest every prayer
And saves us from our foes,
Deliver now Thy little flock
From hymns nobody knows.

In the short time that I taught school, I gleaned enough material to write a column called "The Light Touch" for the *National Education Association Journal.* Here is a column about all those winter clothes small children wear to school:

THE SNOW CHILD

The nine o'clock bell had just rung. The girls were screaming about a spider on Janet's desk; the boys were dropping snowballs in the turtle pond; the custodian wanted to know why I had parked my car by the delivery entrance; the principal was asking for last week's attendance report.

At that precise moment, a bundle of flannel and wool appeared in the doorway and announced it was going to die unless somebody took its snowsuit off. Its fur hat was bound to its head by a wool scarf which was tucked tightly down under the jacket. The jacket was wedged under the suspenders of the snow pants, which were tucked into two shiny red boots, whose buckles were stuck.

I hoisted the creature to a table top and began to work on the buckles. I broke a fingernail, a hair pin, and the points of my scissors.

"I'm going to faint," said the bundle of flannel and wool.
I pulled off the boots and spattered my skirt with mud.

The custodian came back and said my car was blocking the milk truck. I got my purse and gave him the car keys.

"You're not hurrying fast enough," said a voice from under the coonskin cap.

I got the suspenders off and the snow pants and started to work on the jacket, which had been pinned at the collar from underneath. Someone opened the window and an icy blast scattered the attendance sheets on my desk. I rushed to pick them up and stopped a boy who was going to fry Janet's spider on the radiator.

"Only one more minute and I will be dead," said the bundle of flannel and wool. Finally the jacket came off; the mittens came off; the scarf came off; the coonskin cap came off. There stood a pupil from across the hall.

"Thank you," he said, collecting his garments. "I couldn't ask my teacher. She was feeding the fish."

When I was twenty-three years old, something happened that was so sad and terrifying that many years passed before I was able to write about it at all. One day, while we were living in Chicago, my husband suddenly showed signs of severe mental illness; he believed that the professors at the university were trying to kill him. For the next three years, while we moved from state to state, hospital to hospital, looking for a

The illustration for "The Snow Child" that appeared in the *NEA Journal.*

cure, I wrote in earnest and in panic to support us. Sometimes I would take a whole afternoon and go off to a remote spot just to brainstorm—writing down ideas however they occurred to me until finally I had a list of plots to see me through the next few months.

Not all of the ideas were workable, of course, but I was able to use enough of them to pay the rent and buy our food. Unfortunately, my husband did not recover, even with the best of doctors, and after our divorce, I went back to college again for my bachelor's degree, studying to be a clinical psychologist. If I couldn't help my former husband, I thought, perhaps I could help other people before they became so seriously disturbed. I was able to pay a large share of the tuition by writing and selling stories. Finally, however, when I got the degree, I realized that I could never be satisfied unless I wrote full-time, so I gave up plans to go to graduate school and began writing five or six hours a day.

Later, after I married again and became a mother, I began another column about family life, called "The Last Stanza," for the adult church magazines. When I first started writing it, I discovered that using the real names of my husband and children seemed to limit what I could say. I kept wondering if my family would be offended when I poked fun at them, so it was impossible to let my imagination run loose. I solved the problem by changing all our names except my own. My husband, Rex, became Ralph in the series, Jeff became Jack, Michael became Peter, and I invented an imaginary daughter named Susan to round out the family.

My life was settling down at last and I was happy. I was a full-time, freelance writer, and my range of topics was expanding. So was my list of magazines, with names like *Woodmen of the World, The Gospel Trumpet, Hand in Hand, The New York Mirror, Teaching Tools,* and *Elementary English.* I was writing both funny and serious stories, as well as plays, articles, and poems. I was writing for kindergarten children as well as for retired people. But it took four years of full-time writing before I got up the courage to attempt the one thing I had been too terrified to try: a book.

5

From Paragraphs to Chapters

One reason that writing a book frightened me was that I thought I would be bored with it long before I was through. I thought that all books took at least a year or two to write, and if they did not, they weren't any good. What if I spent two years on a book that never sold? What if halfway through I discovered that I simply could not stand the people I was writing about?

Consequently, my first attempt at a book, in 1964, was simply a collection of some of my short stories which had already been published in magazines. It was a safe investment of time. All I had to do was choose the ones I wanted to include and type them up in book form, with the publishers' permission, of course. The first publisher to whom I sent it accepted—miraculously—and the following year *The Galloping Goat and Other Stories* was published by Abingdon Press.

But I was still scared, so I made up another collection, this time of already-published stories for teenagers, *Grasshoppers in the Soup.* It was published in paperback by Fortress Press.

Perhaps I was ready, I thought, to tackle a real honest-to-goodness book, with chapters and everything. Since our family went to the ocean every year, I decided to write a family story that took place in a boardinghouse on the beach. I would approach each chapter as a short story so that the book would not seem such an enormous undertaking.

It worked. I did not get bored with my characters. But I made a mistake that many beginning writers make: I blush to admit that I actually sat down and made a long list of everything exciting that could possibly happen at the ocean—ghosts, mysterious strangers, gypsies, hurricanes, stowaways, you name it—and then divided the whole mess up into chapters. I thought that this book had absolutely every-

The jacket for *The Galloping Goat and Other Stories*, illustration by
Robert L. Jefferson.

thing in it that children could ever want, and I got so enamored of my effort that I sent it off to a publisher who was offering a prize for the best first novel accepted that year.

I did not win the prize. In fact, the manuscript was rejected. But the editor saw possibilities in it. It needed more of a central theme, she said. If I would completely rewrite it from the viewpoint of one character rather than the whole family, she would consider it again. Not buy it, necessarily—just consider it.

My first reaction when I read her letter was that what she wanted was impossible. But the more I thought about it, the more I realized that she was right. Here was my chance to prove that I could do it. So I rewrote the entire book. It took seven months, but after I finally sent it off, back came a contract and a check. *What the Gulls Were Singing* was published by Follett in 1967. It was not an exceptional book, but at least it was publishable.

I began writing one or two books a year. Some, such as *Wrestle the Mountain* (Follett, 1971), about a coal-mining family in West Virginia, or *To Walk the Sky Path* (Follett, 1973), about a Seminole Indian boy in Florida, took most of a year because they required a great deal of

What the Gulls were Singing

Phyllis Reynolds Naylor

Illustration by Ted Lewin from *What the Gulls Were Singing*, published by the Follett Publishing Company.

Illustration by Paul Giovanopoulus from *Wrestle the Mountain*, published by the Follett Publishing Company.

Illustration by Jack Endewelt from *To Walk the Sky Path*, published by the Follett Publishing Company.

research, including travel to both these regions. Others, such as *Making It Happen* (Follett, 1970) and *No Easy Circle* (Follett, 1972), both about teenagers who run away, were so well formed in my mind when I started to write that they were completed within a few months. *Making It Happen* came easily because the main character was actually the same person I had been writing about in my "First Person Singular" columns.

No Easy Circle was not too difficult to write, either, because in many ways the main character, Shelley, was me. When I was in my teens and early twenties, though I never ran away, I had no real concept of who I was or what my abilities were. I wanted to be liked by whatever group I was with at the moment. It wasn't until my late twenties, when I began to feel comfortable about myself, that I realized how much easier it would have been if I had had a role model—some person I wanted to pattern my life after. This, then, became Shelley's battle in the book, and I knew exactly how she felt.

A year before I wrote the book, I had read a series of articles in the *Washington Post* about runaway teenagers from the suburbs who hung around Dupont Circle in Washington, D.C. The articles described the difficulties these people had in adjusting. One paragraph in particular started me thinking seriously of a novel:

"Most of these kids come from fairly nice homes," Officer Buono notes, "and they get unhappy on the street very fast. A girl who has brushed her teeth every morning and lived in a comfortable place, she's going to be disillusioned by ripped mattresses, bugs on the floor, and a bunch of guys saying she has to sleep with them. And she's going to be scared, too."

I knew then that my story was going to be about such a girl, a sensitive girl who will somehow find the courage to say she wants out. In the same article, however, I found the model for Pogo, her friend, because, despite all the disadvantages, some girls decide to stay.

What was it that would make a girl want to stay? What would happen if I placed two girls with very different goals in the same story? What happens to someone with no real concept of who she is? Where does she get the courage to trust herself, to be herself, whatever that is?

I had originally called the book "Vagabond Sunday" which, for a number of reasons, was a dreadful title. The editor said we would have to change it, and she suggested a few new ones. I did not care for her choices, so I sent her a list of my own, which she in turn rejected. Here is the complete list of titles we considered:

The Circle

Follow the Circle

Circle Searcher

At the End of the Circle

To the End of the Circle

Looking for a Lady

Search

Mirror of Myself

From the Mad Scene of Shelley Elizabeth Greer

Circle Watcher

Copping Out

The Saintly Circus

Change in the Wind

Circus Parade

Round and Round She Goes

The Secret Self

I'm Shelley

Ring Around the Circle

Looking for Pogo

Circling, Circling

Shelley's Pogo

Kaleidoscope

Focus
Shelley's Circle
Shelley's Other World
Shelley's Scene
Pogo Panic
Pogo's Scene
Scene at the Circle
Circling the Circle
In Pogo's Place
In Pogo's Power
The Power of Pogo
In Place of Pogo

We were getting nowhere fast. In fact, we were getting positively dizzy. Finally the book salesmen at Follett decided that if there was going to be any title at all, they would have to choose it, so they decided on *No Easy Circle.* Both my editor and I liked it instantly.

Between the books that required a lot of research and books that required none were the ones that often needed strange bits of information to complete a paragraph or chapter. Here are a few of the phone calls I've had to make:

The Civil Aeronautics Board to find out to what altitude a plane rises when taking off from Santa Fe.

69

The jacket for *No Easy Circle*, illustration by Lou Aronson.

A dentist to find out how long dental records are kept.

A lawyer to find out the steps in prosecuting someone for income tax evasion.

A family service agency to ask how they handle cases of child abuse.

An ophthalmologist to ask about the treatment of crossed eyes.

An undertaker to find out how long a wooden casket would last six feet under.

I found that books often had begun to take shape years before I actually wrote them; little incidents came together one by one until eventually they fit together like pieces in a puzzle. *To Make a Wee Moon* (Follett, 1969) began with an old Scottish lullaby that a man had once sung to me many years before. The first verse went like this:

> *Auld Daddie Darkness*
> *Creeps fra' his hole,*
> *Black as a blackamoor,*
> *Blind as a mole.*
> *Stir the fire till it glows,*
> *Let the bairnie sit,*
> *Auld Daddie Darkness*
> *Is not wanted yit.*

I combined the idea of the lullaby with a Scottish superstition I had once read about a ghost-horse called a kelpie. If a kelpie calls your name, it induces you to climb on its back so it can take you down under the water, and you are never seen again.

Then I mixed up both the lullaby and the superstition with memories of a year I once spent on my maternal grandmother's farm in Waverly, Iowa. I changed the location from Iowa to Oshkosh, Wisconsin, however, because I wanted to start out the story with a little ditty that went:

> *There was an old lady from Oshkosh*
> *Who smothered us both with a washcloth.*

By the time this book was published, I had a dozen books under my name as well as several hundred short stories. But one of the most difficult things I had to learn was to look at my own writing as an editor would see it.

6

Through an Editor's Eyes

It was never easy for me to look at my writing from another person's point of view. But my editor had to see things as she knew thousands of readers were going to see them. Had I thought that the readers knew more about a subject than they did? Was the plot contrived? Were the characters well motivated to do what they did? Most of what I learned, I learned from my editors, though I did not always agree with them. Sometimes, especially with my early books, I put up quite an argument.

The climactic scene in *To Make a Wee Moon* involved Jean McGinnis, the daughter of a poor Scottish couple in search of a house, discovering the possibilities for a home in an old abandoned schoolhouse. This is what the editor, Paula Orellana, had to say:

It is a fine sensitive family story and even without my half Scots-Irish ancestry, I would be charmed by the characters and the background. But there are several points I would like to discuss. First, the discovery of the school for a home by Jean. I think it would strengthen the character of Angus, as father and provider, if he were the one who found the empty school as a possible home. It would seem a logical and more realistic solution in that he has supposedly been spending entire days in search of a house and land in the area. He may have heard it discussed as a hazard for children who play there alone or as a stopping place for vagrants or some other device to make him more aware of it and its possibilities.

To which I indignantly replied:

It would probably strengthen the character of the father were he the one to discover the school, but I'm afraid it would ruin the whole theme of the book. The point of the story is that Jean, when the story begins, rebels bitterly against the economic status of her family and is somewhat obsessed by the things she can't have. It is only slowly, through her relationship with Aunt Gwen, that she begins to see the simple beauty and the unusual possibilities in the common things around her—the possibilities in her own dresses, in old pear boxes, and even in Donald Harvie, whom Jean had quickly dismissed as an uninteresting, silent farmhand. The very climax of the book is that, in time of family crisis, it is Jean who has matured enough, with her aunt's help, to see the possibilities in an old schoolhouse, and so save the day for her family. This, I feel, is far more important to young readers than whether her father is or isn't a very strong character. I don't mean to excuse poor writing on my part if Big Angus comes across as a weak man, but feel that the readers are far more interested in Jean. Do you understand my point? The book is centered around Jean's struggle to accept what life gives her and use it as creatively as possible, and she is finally able to do this when she sees a schoolhouse as a home. To have her father steal this scene cheats the readers, in my opinion.

But finally, with the editor's next letter, I gave in, perhaps only because I was outnumbered:

I certainly do understand your point of Jean's maturing slowly through the book and finally seeing things for more than their face value. You have deftly shown this through, as you say, the dollhouse, the dress, Donald, and her final reaction to Brother Bean. I really feel this shines through very well without the added unrealistic climactic touch. If Jean can see

The jacket for *To Make a Wee Moon,* illustration by Beth and Joe Krush.

*and exclaim about the possibilities of her father's announce-
ment of the school for a home, she will show maturity in the
same way—and just as convincingly as if she had discovered it
herself. She still would be accepting what life gives her and
using it as creatively as possible by accepting her father's sug-
gestion, which is by no means scene stealing. Please believe
that we are both equally interested in making this the best
possible book. There were four readers from the editorial
department here who independently read your manuscript
and commented on this same point as being unrealistic. As
a former book reviewer myself, I feel opinions are often
negative toward children who solve the adult problems of
the book themselves.*

One of the things my editors taught me was
that if I did not believe my plot, no one else
would either. *Witch's Sister* got its start years ago
in the worst nightmare I ever had. I dreamed
that my mother, my own dear, sweet mother,
had had her legs chopped off at the knees. It
didn't seem to have hurt her; it just made her
angry. Around the house she chased me on
those awful bloody stumps—*clump, clump, clump*—
her face hideous, and I screamed in terror as
she came closer. Years later my older son con-
fided to me that *his* worst dream was one in

which he came to ask me a question, and when I turned to answer, I had the face of a horrible witch.

I decided that having a parent become an enemy was one of the most frightening things a child could imagine, and I expanded the idea to include anyone to whom children go for help or protection, anyone who might be in charge.

With this as the theme of *Witch's Sister,* I wrote the book. I had already decided that the ending would be uncertain. I would not tell my readers for sure whether Lynn's older sister, Judith, was or was not a witch. But deep down, I thought that perhaps it was all Lynn's imagination—a psychological twist, a string of coincidences. Back came the manuscript from the editor, Jean Karl, with this note:

> *. . . I am afraid you never really convince me that there was any possibility that Judith was a witch. I always believed that that was a part of Lynn's fertile imagination. . . . If you should ever rewrite your book, I will be glad to take another look.*

I wrote it again. This time I forced myself to cross that line between the world as we know it and the unknown, to rewrite the story convincingly enough so that when I was through, I truly did not know whether or not Judith was up to witchcraft. And Mrs. Tuggle, who before had been merely a somewhat mysterious though genial old woman, now had an air of evil about her that made my flesh creep. In the first draft, Mrs. Tuggle merely puttered about the house with her one green eye and one gray one, recounting witch tales from the north country, speaking of bogles, hobyahs, creeping rivulets of water, and squishy mools. But in the final draft, as lightning flashes and thunder rocks the house, she moves about the darkened living room chanting a poem while shadows twist and touch on the wall behind her:

> *From the shadows of the pool,*
> *Black as midnight, thick as gruel,*
> *Come, my nymphs, and you shall be*
> *Silent images of me.*
>
> *Suck the honey from my lips,*
> *Dance upon my fingertips.*
> *When the darkness tolls the hour*
> *I shall have you in my power.*
>
> *Fast upon us, spirits all,*
> *Listen for our whispered call.*

Illustration by Gail Owens from *Witch's Sister,* published by Atheneum.

Whistling kettle, tinkling bell,
Weave your web and spin your spell.

The book was published in 1975 by Atheneum and was followed by two sequels from the same publisher: *Witch Water* (1977) and *The Witch Herself* (1978), and three additional books published by Delacorte: *The Witch's Eye* (1990), *Witch Weed* (1991), and *The Witch Returns* (1992).

When I wrote my second book for Atheneum, *Walking Through the Dark* (1976), I had a different problem. This story concerned a teenage girl growing up in Chicago during the Depression. This time Jean Karl wrote:

We do see Ruth growing and developing. We see her rela-
tionships changing. But we do not see enough of what Ruth is
seeing of the world. We need to know a little bit more about
her hopes and plans in the end for us to see completely what
has happened to her. In the beginning she is a carefree girl
who cares most about going to the movies on Saturday,
clothes, and boys. Her ideas change, but we are not quite sure
what they change to. . . .

I thought a long time about Ruth. I decided that the reason I had not developed her character more was that I did not really like her in the first place. I had portrayed her as shallow and selfish, without acknowledging that even shallow, selfish people have hopes and fears as well as times when they are genuinely kind. It was not until I filled out Ruth's personality and felt more sympathetic toward her myself that the book seemed to come alive. I learned that if I did not care much for my main character, I could not expect others to care either.

I also discovered that ignorance rarely goes unnoticed. I had lived in Chicago, true, but not during the Depression. Still, secure in the thought that none of my teenage readers would know whether or not I was correct, I portrayed a Chicago neighborhood as I imagined it to have been in the 1930s. Imagine my horror when Jean Karl wrote:

Incidentally, you do happen to be writing about an area that I knew very well as I was growing up. I don't remember it quite as early as your story because I wasn't old enough yet to remember it in detail at this time, but I certainly do remember it from the mid to late '30s, and you will find all through the manuscript questions about your setting. . . .

Illustration by James and Ruth McCrea from *Walking Through the Dark,* published by Atheneum.

So much for sloppy research.

I soon found that it was not only the reaction of readers I had to be concerned about, but the people who would review my book for journals and newspapers, because many librarians and bookstores rely on reviews when deciding what to purchase. When I first began writing books, it was hard to remember that it was no more realistic to believe that everyone would like my books than it was to believe that everyone would like rhubarb pie.

Here are two of the reviews of *To Make a Wee Moon*:

Gr 4–6—A slow-moving, mediocre story about two children who are sent to their grandmother's Wisconsin farm until their parents can gather their resources to join them, and who find themselves in a thoroughly miserable situation. An ungentle grandmother whose life is ruled by the fairies she imported from Scotland, a mannish aunt who finally elopes with the umambitious hired man, and a small assortment of preachers, teachers, and carnival barkers present an unattractive but no doubt realistic picture of rural life an unspecified number of years ago. "To make a wee moon," Aunt Gwen keeps saying, "all we need is a little patience and a lot of hard work." Patience and hard work abound, but little real interest, and most girls will wonder if the resulting "wee moon" was worth quite so much moralizing.—Katherine Heylman, Sunview Elementary School Library, Lyndhurst, Ohio

*   *   *

Illustrated by Beth and Joe Krush. Skill in developing a picture of rural Wisconsin life and a remarkably acute recalling of childhood feelings give notable reality to this family story. From the opening, when Jean and young Brian take a long train ride from West Virginia coal country to Grandmother's farm, to the conclusion, when father and mother at last find land on which to make their own way, the story has a ring of truth. Each person is clearly individualized: Grandmother (from Skye) who "had the look of a troll about her" (she does believe in the wee folk); Donald Harvie, the hired man, who elopes with Aunt Gwen to become "Uncle" to Jean; creative Aunt Gwen, who helps Jean make a most ingenious doll's house; Preacher Bean in his revival tent gaining crowds as he talks against the sins of Mr. Murray's carnival; and abandoned Tommy Pepper, whose effect on all—including schoolmates—is a remarkable, salutary one. Their problems, presented more openly than in some such stories, become part of Jean's growing up. She realizes that it is "possible to like a person partly and partly not like him at all." A rewarding book. V.H., The Horn Book.

At first, reviews, whether good or bad, affected me more than they should have. If it was a stunning review, it was easy to feel—for an hour, perhaps—that I was a much better writer than I was. If it was a slashing attack, it was tempting to give up. The only cure for either, I found, was to get involved immediately in another writing project, to spend every available minute planning a new book. Then the problem became one of trying to find all those minutes and hours and days necessary for writing, because it was always the *next* book, I thought, that would be my very best.

7

Taking Time

There is an old story about a beggar who begged not for spare coins but spare minutes. I often feel that way. When I married the second time, I had no trouble writing at least a little every day. It was easy to slip out for lunch with my new husband or to spend an hour shopping for a lamp, because if I didn't write in the morning, there was always the afternoon. And if not the afternoon, I could always write in the evening.

I didn't get truly organized until I became a mother and found that babies are not content to lie on their backs and coo. I cherished what little time I had left for myself. The moment the children were in bed for their naps, I started writing, and later, when they entered school,

The jacket for *Eddie, Incorporated,* illustration by Blanche Sims.

my "office hours" began the moment they were out of the house and stopped when they got home. I could always make beds while I listened to elephant jokes, but I couldn't rewrite the fourth paragraph on page seven.

I need to work without interruption. I can write in restaurants or hotel lobbies or train stations where there is a lot of noise and confusion, provided I feel sure that no one will talk to me. But it's hard to write in a perfectly quiet house if I think I'm likely to be interrupted.

Once, when I was speaking to a high school creative-writing class and told them that I write for five or six hours each day, a girl said, "But writers aren't supposed to be like that! They're only supposed to write when they're inspired!"

It's true that each story or book begins in a burst of enthusiasm, but once I start, I need to write on a daily schedule. This is something I learned to do with practice.

I used to worry a lot about how other writers went about their work. Eudora Welty was supposed to have taken sixteen years to write her novel *Losing Battles*, and Katherine Anne Porter twenty years to write *Ship of Fools.* Lore Segal, it was said, took seven years to write the 177 pages of her book *Lucinella,* and she wrote every day of the week. That meant twenty-five pages a year, or two pages a month, or a half-page a week, or about two lines per day! If I finshed writing a book in less than a year, could it possibly be any good?

Gradually I stopped worrying so much about what famous writers were doing and set my own pace. Now I sometimes write rapidly and other times not very fast at all. Some books require considerable patience and others seem to come off the top of my head. The number of pages often has little to do with it. *Eddie, Incorporated,* 101 pages, based on some of the "businesses" my younger son once tried, and the zany book *How Lazy Can You Get?,* fifty pages, about those weird questions adults ask children ("How stupid can you be?" "How messy can you get?"), were each written in only a few months' time. But the picture book *Old Sadie and the Christmas Bear* took longer than either one of these, even though it had only twenty-nine pages, and half of those were pictures. Picture books take the longest for me to write because every word has to be chosen so carefully. Sometimes I put a picture book manuscript away for months or even years, then get it out again and work on it some more.

The most important thing, I've found, is

The jacket for *Old Sadie and the Christmas Bear*, illustration by Patricia Montgomery Newton.

never, never to turn in a manuscript unless I feel it is the very best I can do—until I can't find a single paragraph or line that I think can be changed for the better. While one part of me wants to take the time to write the best book I know how, another part of me wants to hurry and get it done, to see if the ending comes out the way I wanted it to. It's so easy to trick myself into reading rapidly over the paragraphs that aren't quite right, pretending that they are "good enough." If there is something unresolved in my plot, however—something so small I think no one will notice—I have learned this: Someone will notice. When I turn in a manuscript with "gray" areas in it, patches of the story that are a shade below the rest, these are exactly the ones that my editor will ask me about.

The first sentence, the first paragraph, and the first page of a book are, for me, the most difficult. There are times I spend days on the first paragraph alone because this sets the tone and style for the rest of the book. Once I succeed in capturing exactly what I'm after, then the other chapters go much more smoothly. But if I'm unsure of the mood and the writing is sloppy, I usually have to throw the whole chapter out and start over.

Taking time means being willing not only to write slowly and carefully—six, seven, or eight drafts, if necessary—but to resist rushing a book off to the publisher once it's done. *Ice* (Atheneum, 1995) went through *eighteen* revisions before I got it right. I've learned to let a manuscript sit for a few days or weeks—a year, even—then read it again, looking for places that might be improved. I've also discovered the value of reading my work aloud to a small group of writer friends for their comments. Even reading aloud to myself helps me pick up rough places in the rhythm and wording that I hadn't caught before.

Finally, when I feel that a manuscript is the best I can possibly do, I turn it over to my husband, who happens to be very good at editing. So good, in fact, that he has read and commented on all of my books before they were published.

This is usually hard on both of us, however. I often sit across the room from him, watching over the top of the newspaper. If he frowns even once, I worry. If the pages seem to turn rapidly without too many marks of his pencil, I'm encouraged. If he yawns, I am filled with despair, but if he laughs aloud, I'm ecstatic.

Even though I beg him to be honest, there are times when his criticism is so discouraging that I speak only when spoken to for a day or so. He usually proves to be right, however, and I wonder how it is that I can't see the faults in a story myself. Always, when I have finally finished a manuscript after five or six drafts, I look at the final version and think, Why didn't the words come to me like that in the first place?

I know that every job, even tap dancing or opera singing has something about it that isn't fun. The part about writing that I don't enjoy is correcting galley proofs, those loose sheets of paper on which the book is first printed so that the typesetting can be checked for errors. In this laborious process, every word, every punctuation mark, has to be looked over carefully, to make sure that all is correct before the final printing. A proofreader does the same with his own copy of the galleys back in the copyeditor's office.

No matter how hard we all try, however, it seems that one or two errors usually squeak through. Sometimes when the printer corrects one mistake, he inadvertently makes a new one. One of the funniest mistakes in something of mine was in a magazine story called, "The Twelve Days of Christmas." The very last line

Rex and Phyllis Naylor.
"He reads every manuscript before it is submitted and makes corrections."

was supposed to read, "Marvin Migglesby sat by the fire roasting chestnuts and feeding them to the dog." But when the story came out, I was horrified to read, "Marvin Migglesby sat by the fire roasting the dog."

How could it be, I've often wondered, that I actually chose this job? I've never been known for patience. I've never been a perfectionist, either. I was always terrible in subjects like arithmetic, which required a precise answer. I played the piano but never understood beats and measures, so I just made up the timing as I went along; if I came to a difficult passage, I skipped over it. How could I possibly have ended up scrutinizing every word and quotation mark on a set of galleys?

Because stories have a way of haunting me, I feel restless when a story is churning inside my head. The only cure is to get words down on paper.

The jacket for *The Keeper*, illustration by Ronald Himler.

8

The Haunting

There's no other way to describe it: a news story, something I've seen, or a brutal injustice shown on TV will move into my head. It will stay uninvited for weeks . . . months . . . years, even, and haunt me until I do something about it. For a writer, that means write. What if . . . ? the writer asks herself, and so begins a new story.

After the mental illness of my first husband, I thought about how difficult it had been for me, a young wife. I wondered how I would have coped if I were a thirteen-year-old boy, perhaps, just starting to make friends in a new school. How would he have handled an unpredictable father who did strange things in the middle of the night and made it impossible to invite friends home? I wrote *The Keeper* because I had to know.

I strongly believe that writing keeps me sane. When our family visited the Rockies, our two sons—young men, by then—decided to climb Longs Peak. Since I am afraid of heights, but knew I could not change their minds, I realized that this would be one of the most difficult days of my life. Only by concentrating on a new book could I get through it. And so I began the first chapter of *The Fear Place*, about two brothers in the Rockies. They were not our sons, to be sure, but somehow having four boys to worry about instead of only two helped dilute my fear of what could be happening up there on the mountain.

When a worry becomes an idea, the idea a haunting, and the haunting at last becomes a book, the process usually happens over a period of many months, sometimes years. But *Shiloh* didn't begin that way. Having discovered a young, abused dog in Shiloh, West Virginia, on a visit to friends, I was haunted by the worry of what might become of the little dog. Finally my husband said, "Are you going to have a nervous breakdown, Phyllis, or are you going to do

Mike and Jeff Naylor point toward the summit of Longs Peak in the Rockies after their successful climb. It was this event that sparked the idea for the writing of *The Fear Place*.

something about it?" And so began the story of Shiloh, all other projects pushed aside.

Three weeks into the writing of my book, we heard from our friends in West Virginia that the dog was still there, and so they adopted her and named her Clover. But that didn't stop my story. What if . . . ? I had already asked myself. "What if an abused dog ran away from its legal owner and came to me? What would I do?" And then the next question: "If I were eleven years old, what would I do?"

The crazy thing was, after I won the Newbery Medal for this book, the shy, trembling little dog in West Virginia became a celebrity. Our friends received phone calls from as far away as Denver promising to pay all expenses if they would just put the dog on a plane and fly her out to their school or library so readers could see the real Shiloh. Our friends did not do that, but they did, on request, take her around to schools and libraries in West Virginia to be petted and admired, and report that she loved all the attention.

A happy ending, yes, but it did not stop the haunting. It was not just the dog who was a ghostly presence in my head, but the villain, Judd Travers. What might have happened in such a man's life to rob him so of self-esteem that he would take his anger out on a helpless dog? I wondered. *Shiloh Season* was written next, followed by *Saving Shiloh,* to complete the trilogy.

Oftentimes it is not one climactic episode that inspires the writing of a book, but rather bits and pieces picked up here and there, such as newspaper accounts of racists tying a black man to a truck and dragging him to his death; of the beating of a gay college student in Wyoming; or the Neo-Nazis celebrating Hitler's birthday. Predictions of terrible things to come in the year 2000, and the dangers of allowing immigrants into our country, or of allowing any type of gun control—all these fears. How do these hatreds and fears begin? I asked myself, and I wrote *Walker's Crossing* to find the answer, to work it out on paper.

To be a true haunting, I suppose, there should be a real ghost, and—next to my witch books—*Jade Green: A Ghost Story,* has got to be one of the creepiest books I've written. If a supposedly sad story doesn't bring tears to my eyes when I write it, it won't make the reader cry. If a scene doesn't make me laugh out loud, then I know it's not funny enough for the reader. When I wrote some of the chapters in *Jade Green*

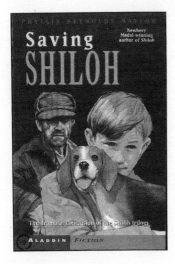

The jackets for the *Shiloh* trilogy, illustrations by Barry Moser.

and felt the skin on my arms turn to goose flesh, I felt satisfied that perhaps readers would feel the same way.

How strange it is that, in a physical sense, all stories are, really, are little black marks on white paper, and yet they have the power to move us to laughter or reduce us to tears. Because I like the idea of making something out of nothing, I love the arts. The artist, with nothing more than paint and a brush, creates a masterpiece. The sculptor with his hands and a lump of clay produces a figure. But the writer needs nothing more than the stub of a pencil and some old scraps of paper to create fear and rage and sorrow and joy. Why would I ever want to do anything else?

9

The Spark

"Okay," said a friend. "You have an idea, but how exactly do you *start* a book? What do you do first?"

There seems to be some notion that if writing could be reduced to steps one through ten, like a recipe, you could open the oven door at the end and take out a finished book. Or, at the very least, if you got off to a proper start, you could automatically follow through. That's the scary part about being a writer. There's no guarantee that, even if you put in a fifteen-hour day, you're going to accomplish anything at all.

If I were baking bread or weaving a rug, I would know when I got up in the morning that if I followed my instructions carefully, I would have something to show for it at the end of the day. I might be tired from having come home late the night before, or I might be worried about a member of my family, but the bread would be baked or the rug would be woven.

As a writer, however, I'm always conscious of the time when I go out for the evening. I know that if my mind is to function the next day, I have to be alert, and that if I am upset over something, it will be hard to concentrate. With every new book, there is an awful mixture of anticipation and terror; I am wildly excited by what I want to do, but there is absolutely no assurance that I will be able to do it. It doesn't matter how many books I have written or what prizes they might have won. A new book is always a gamble.

Because I got my start writing for church magazines, I often typed up twenty copies of one story and sent it to twenty different publications. Since Catholics didn't usually read Protestant church magazines, and Baptists didn't read Methodist publications, the editors did not mind that a story was being published in many different places. And because I wrote short stories for fifteen years before I ever attempted a novel, I have had published almost two thousand stories, poems, and articles. Many more were rejected than accepted, of course, but even I was astounded at the number of rejections to date: 5,971 acceptances; 10,335 rejections. A writer must, if anything, be thick-skinned.

While one book may require only one hand-written draft before it goes onto the word processor, another may require many, many drafts in longhand before it ever gets to that stage. While working from an outline might be best for one story, another might do better with no outline at all. But even if the mechanics, the nitty-gritty of writing, were the same for all books and all authors, there is a certain spark that is necessary to bring a book to life, and that is the most difficult of all to explain.

I know, by an overwhelming feeling of excitement, when I'm ready to begin a new book. This is more than just thinking, *Now that's a nice idea!* There is a notebook beside my chair filled with book ideas, but for the moment, that's all they are: just ideas. At some point, however, after something I've read or something I've dreamed or something I remember from the past, I think, *I could do something special with that idea!* I see a way to bring a bit of myself to a plot, to contribute something that is uniquely mine. It's this that starts the excitement.

The title of this new book-to-be is now printed on a piece of masking tape, then stuck on a three-ring notebook. It will take its place among other notebooks beside my chair, each filled with character-sketches, plot summaries, news clippings, photos, maps, and scribbled notes to myself, all of which I will use in the actual writing. I may continue to collect things for months or even years.

The Agony of Alice began to "grow" when I remembered playing Tarzan with a neighborhood boy when I was eight. I was Jane, and at some point in my script, he was supposed to kiss me, but I collapsed in embarrassment whenever he got within a foot of my face.

I began thinking of all the other things I had done that were silly or stupid, and how fervently I hoped that whoever had seen me do them had forgotten them by now or was dead. I knew, as most writers discover sooner or later, that whatever has happened to me, no matter how humiliating or unusual it seemed at the time, has usually happened to others as well. And so I

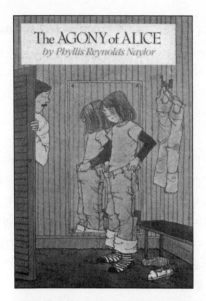

The jackets for *The Agony of Alice*, illustration by Blanche Sims, and *Achingly Alice*, illustration by Kam Mak.

became tremendously excited with the idea of a funny book about a girl named Alice and all the agonies she suffers when she remembers the embarrassing things that have happened to her. The book begins with Alice talking.

The summer between fifth and sixth grades, something happens to your mind. With me, the box of Crayolas did it— thirty-two colors, including copper and burgundy. I was putting them in a sack for our move to Silver Spring when I remembered how I used to eat crayons in kindergarten.

I didn't just eat them, either. One day when I was bored I stuck two crayons up my nostrils, then leaned over my desk and wagged my head from side to side like an elephant with tusks, and the teacher said, "Alice McKinley, what on earth are you doing?"

As a matter of fact, I never stuck crayons up my nose, but I saw a boy do it in third grade, and I remember thinking, *Now that is the stupidest thing I have ever seen, and I'll remember it all my life.* And I have. But it merely reminds me that perhaps other people are remembering all the ridiculous things that *I've* done, and the only way to feel better about that is to laugh.

When I wrote the first Alice book, I had no idea there would be others. Then letters from readers began to arrive, begging for more, and reviewers wrote things like, "Alice's fans await her further adventures." *What?* I said. And so the Alice series was born. She is older in each book, and I plan twenty-eight books in all, the last one taking Alice from age eighteen to her sixtieth birthday.

For some books, it takes a long time for the spark to kindle. Many years ago, I read a magazine article that said that the three most popular words in book titles for children are *horse, mystery,* and *secret.* The writer went on to say, tongue-in-cheek, that if an author wanted to write the all-time favorite children's book, it should be called "The Secret Mystery Horse." I filed this away in the back of my mind.

A few years later I thought, *Why not?* Why not write a good mystery that involves a horse? My only experience with horses, however, other than seeing them from a distance on the farm, is that when I was a freshman in high school, I enrolled in a riding class that met on Saturday mornings. I didn't want to ride horses nearly as much as I wanted to wear jodhpurs like the rich girls who lived on the west side of town.

The first thing I discovered was that I looked terrible in jodhpurs. The next thing I found

Phyllis Naylor's *Night Cry* won an Edgar Allan Poe award in 1985 for best children's mystery book of the year. Jacket painting by Ruth Sanderson.

was that I was terrified of horses. Every week I went to that stable in a state of dread. And because I was content to take the horse slowly around the ring, the instructor would come over from time to time and hit the horse on its hindquarters, forcing it into a trot. I would cling to the mane and pray for deliverance. That was all I knew about horses. So I asked myself, Why not write about a girl, then, who is terrified of horses, or perhaps of a certain horse?

Now I was feeling excited, because I could see myself in the story. There was still the problem of writing about horses when I didn't know much about them. I realized that the only way I could handle this was to keep the horse in the background while still making it an important part of the book. I decided to do this by having the girl suspect the horse of being a demon. I would hold this terror continually over the reader's head while conveniently keeping the horse itself safely behind the fence in the pasture. So much for the horse.

All the while the anticipation builds about a book-to-be, I am getting a sense of the mood of the story. I wanted to place this story somewhere that would contribute to a mood of loneliness and isolation.

My father and his people were from Mississippi. They weren't city people, but lived out in the backwoods. The trips we had taken to visit them clung to me over the years like the moss that hung on the trees, and now the story began to grow right before my eyes. I would place my characters in the hill country of northeastern Mississippi. The mood was complete when I decided that I would make the girl's father in the story a calendar sales- man, as my own father had been for a time. Although my father was more sophisticated than Ellen April's in the book, I had met enough of his relatives over the years to feel very much at home with them, and could easily put myself in their little dogtrot cabin on five acres of land. At this point, I was ready to begin the book, to shape the plot, and I no longer cared about making it "an all-time favorite." Instead of "The Secret Mystery Horse," I called my book *Night Cry*. It begins:

Fear, like icy pellets, rained down on her as Ellen entered the barn. In the sudden darkness she could not see him, but she knew that Sleet was there.

Any number of things can spark enthusiasm

in me for an idea. It isn't always a character that excites me first, like Alice McKinley in *The Agony of Alice,* or the mood cast by the demon horse in *Night Cry.* Sometimes it is simply the situation. In one of my fantasy novels, *Sang Spell,* Josh Vardy, who has been beaten and robbed while hitchiking to Texas, awakens to find himself in a village from which there is seemingly no escape. And sometimes the spark begins not with a character or plot or situation, but with a theme, the "meaning" of a book. The three books of my York Trilogy, *Shadows on the Wall, Faces in the Water,* and *Footprints at the Window,* focus on how we deal with uncertainty. Dan Roberts must go back in time to the Roman conquests and the Black Death to see how other civilizations faced a troubled future, in order to come to terms with the possibility that he may have inherited a fatal disease.

For me, a book seems pointless unless the main character changes in some way. This doesn't mean there will always be a happy ending. It doesn't even mean that the character need change for the better. But if nothing happens during the story that is different from any other time, and the protagonist is exactly the same at the end as he was at the

The Grand Escape, illustration by Alan Daniel.

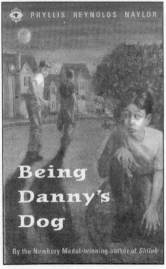

The jackets for *The Solomon System,* illustration by Ronald Himler, and *Being Danny's Dog,* illustration by Gabriela Dellosso.

beginning, the reader may well ask, "So what?"

When I start work on a new book, I know how it will begin, how it will end, and a few of the things that will happen along the way. I also have a good idea of what the climactic scene will be—the turning point in the plot, so to speak. In *Night Cry* it is Ellen's hair-raising rescue with the horse she once feared; in *The Keeper* it is Nick's realization that he must let go of his closely guarded secret about his father.

Other than these specific guideposts, however, the rest of the plot is usually something of a mystery, as though I am walking through a maze, and little things happen that surprise and delight me. Sometimes I seem to be leading my characters and other times they are leading me, but if I try to make them do anything that is not absolutely right for them, the writing becomes laborious and the magic goes out of the page. Then I have to stop, go back, and get in touch with them again.

When I first began writing, it was hard enough to put characters, theme, and plot together without trying to complicate them in any way. But half the fun of writing is to bring out several different sides of a personality and to weave subplots in and around the main plot, tying them together in the end. While the main plot in *Night Cry* is the kidnapping and rescue, for example, there are subplots of gossip in the small mountain community and what it can lead to, of the retarded boy's struggle for acceptance, and of Ellen's need to break out of her shyness and experience more of the world. The deeper I dig into my story, the more I enjoy writing it.

Some books seem to spawn others. The characters of Ted and Nory from *The Solomon System*, appear in different disguises in my Danny books—*Being Danny's Dog* and *Danny's Desert Rats.* They are younger in these books, and their names and families have changed, but I liked the original relationship between the brothers, and hated to let them go.

The Grand Escape was written, quite honestly, for revenge. After one of our cats greedily swallowed a large quantity of crinkle ribbon, requiring an operation that cost me $450, I was determined to get my money back for all the damage our two cats had cost us. So I wrote a book about them. I had so much fun in the process, however, that it became a series, and *The Healing of Texas Jake* came next, followed by *Carlotta's Kittens and the Club of Mysteries.* And of course I simply have to cut loose every so often and write another book in my zany Bernie Magruder mystery series, about a boy whose father is caretaker of the Bessledorf Hotel. Or another book in the boys-versus-girls series (*The Boys Start the War, The Girls Get Even,* etc.).

It would be so much easier if book ideas came to me in an orderly fashion, each one waiting its turn. Some of them do. But others descend on me in a hurry, upsetting and exhilarating me, both at the same time. They push their way ahead of the rest, demand to be recognized, and make whatever book I'm working on at the time seem insignificant.

It's always been hard for me to keep my mind on the book at hand. The stack of three-ring notebooks by my chair is growing and I'm sure that on my deathbed I will gasp, "But I still have five more books to write!"

PHYLLIS REYNOLDS NAYLOR

The Treasure of Bessledorf Hill

By the author of the SHILOH trilogy

ALADDIN *MYSTERY*

The jacket for *The Treasure of Bessledorf Hill*, illustration by James Bernardin.

10

The Rock in My Shoe

We come to understand ourselves through what we write. One of the reasons I write—why I need so to write—is because I feel I have so little control over life, certainly over the lives of those close to me. I can't put them in a glass bubble and protect them always. So in my books, I decide what will happen. And yet . . .

In the three books of my York Trilogy—*Shadows on the Wall, Faces in the Water,* and *Footprints at the Window*—Dan still doesn't know, at the very end, whether he carries a hereditary disease; in *The Solomon System,* the parents do separate; in *A String of Chances,* the baby dies; and in *The Keeper,* it is doubtful whether Nick's father will ever recover from his paranoia.

What's the point of having control, then, if art is going to imitate life with all its risks? Because, in each of my stories, I'm working out for myself, and possibly for the reader, how I would react in a similar situation. I'm facing problems on paper, where they aren't quite so threatening, looking for my own strengths, deciding how, and even whether, I could cope.

Those who know me well—certainly my husband and sons—would classify me, I'm sure, as a worrier. A happy worrier, *quite* happy, in fact, but I've always been somewhat anxious. As a child, when I wasn't worried about the Last Judgment (which is why I carried two butter cookies around in my pocket, should I find myself unexpectedly in a long line), I worried about being separated from people I loved. It was my fear of a long freight train stopping on the tracks and separating me from my mother, that made me run in front of one when I was five. In kindergarten, I cried whenever the teacher left the room. Even in my teens, I got homesick when I was away overnight. Yet I was the first child in our family to move out of town, then out of state, and finally across the country.

We change in some ways as we grow older and in other the ways stay the same. The Last

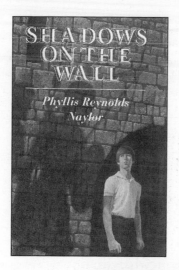
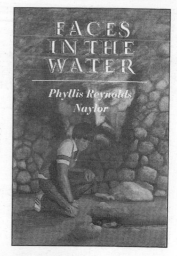
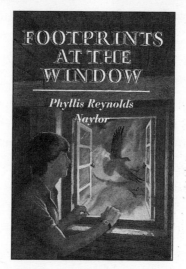

The jackets for the York Trilogy: *Shadows on the Wall; Faces in the Water;* and *Footprints at the Window,* illustrations by Ruth Sanderson.

Judgment no longer keeps me awake nights, I adore trains, and I do not cry for my mother. But I'm still not very comfortable leaving home base. Although we have done quite a lot of traveling as a family, I'm a white-knuckled flyer. When it comes to airplanes, I would prefer to have my entire family with me, so that if we all go down, we go together, and there won't be orphaned children left behind, even though these children are now grown and married!

A psychiatrist once said that people who are afraid to fly are operating on a "what if" basis— what if the engines give out, what if the landing gear won't work, what if . . . what if. . . . But *of course,* I thought. What's so strange about that? That's what writers do all the time; we are always imagining what would happen *if.* That's what it's all about!

Another thing I discovered from my writing is that I use humor as a way of facing problems. The books that are easiest for me to write are the funny ones, and writing *The Agony of Alice* was so enjoyable it was almost like a vacation. I also had a great time writing the picture book *"I Can't Take You Anywhere!"*, about a girl who is sort of a klutz. Whenever possible, I put humor in even

125

my most serious novels, unless I feel it will totally break the mood.

I have also, through my books, come to know my own people. Two things the author Willa Cather once said have stayed with me: "Let your fiction grow out of the land beneath your feet," and "The years from eight to fifteen are the formative period in a writer's life."

Long ago I copied those two sentences down without having any idea, really, of how they applied to me. It wasn't so much that there was nothing to write about back in the Midwest, as that we never seemed to stay in one place long enough to put down roots.

The land beneath *my* feet was constantly changing. In my adult book *Crazy Love*, I wrote:

Mine was the most ordinary family in the entire Midwest. Whenever people wrote about middle-class values, mores, income, or politics, that was my family they were talking about. A walking Norman Rockwell portfolio, that was us. We were descended on both sides from a long line of teachers, preachers, and farmers. My father worked as a salesman for various companies, beginning with H. J. Heinz in the Depression, symbolized by a giant pickle. All through our childhood he was so loyal that I didn't discover Campbell's soups until I was married. As he changed jobs, we changed houses, and by the time I entered high school, we had lived in eight different neighborhoods, stretching across Indiana, Illinois, and Iowa. And that's where our personalities developed. Like the roads in Iowa as seen from a plane, all coming together at perfect right angles, the men and women of American Gothic lived their lives square and true.

In those formative years that Cather wrote about, we frequently vacationed at either one of my grandparents' homes. If we drove west to Iowa, we drove through flat farmland—peaceful horses and contented cows, endlessly chewing. When we got to the farm in Waverly, we would be met at the door by my maternal grandmother, who promptly fed us and put us to bed. Hugs were reserved for arrivals and departures, and in between was the practical, no-nonsense business of the day to attend to, without emotion or fuss.

When I was warned once not to give my baby brother corn for fear he might choke, I took pity on him anyway, and as he toddled up to me at the table, I surreptitiously slipped him a few kernels. My grandmother, noticing, got up from her chair, lifted me up by one arm, gave me a spanking, sat back down, and continued the conversation. No emotion. No fuss.

About my relatives, I wrote in *Crazy Love*:

It was not just the five of us—mother, father, three chil-
dren—who were ordinary, however. Counting all blood rel-
atives on both sides—forty-four aunts, uncles, cousins, and
grandparents—no one had ever been in jail. No one had ever
been arrested, molested, or raped. No one had ever had heart
disease, diabetes, or tuberculosis. No one got his picture in
Look *or* Life. *When two of my uncles founded a manufactur-*
ing company for heavy equipment, we finally had a success
story to recount again and again over the ham and biscuits at
family reunions. And when one of my aunts married a man
who later robbed this company (he was apprehended making
his getaway at seven miles an hour in the huge orange crane he
had stolen), we had a scandal, too, of our very own.

This farm in Iowa was so remote from
neighboring houses that we could see no other
from the front steps. My world was bordered by
cornfields and fences and by the one-room
school, a mile away, where we traipsed when
we stayed one winter. It formed the landscape
for my book *To Make a Wee Moon*, as well as *Beetles,*
Lightly Toasted. Maudie in the Middle, which I
co-authored with my mother, also takes place
in Iowa.

Some summers, however, we did not go west

for vacation, but headed east instead, where the land became mysterious and hilly about the time we reached Pittsburgh. From then on the terrain was rolling, the roads curving, and we would eagerly hang out the car windows, watching for the first sign of Maryland soil, each wanting to be the first child to screech, "Purple dirt!"

Again we arrived late in the evening and were fed and put to bed, but this was a different world from the one back in Iowa. My paternal grandparents, who insisted on being called Pappaw and Mammaw, had come up from Mississippi, and the humid, suffocating climate of inbred warmth and gossip had migrated north along with them. It was said that Pappaw's courtship of Mammaw began when he was a young boy and she just a baby. He would pick her up, carry her about in his arms, and announce proudly, "This is the girl I'm going to marry." And he did, when she was only fifteen. She was playing with her dolls right up to the day of the wedding.

In Iowa, by contrast, my maternal grandfather had started his courtship of my grandmother by sending her a formal letter, written painstakingly, with curled letters, on elegant stationery:

Sunday eve, May 20, 1894
Miss Emma Thompson
Van Horne, Iowa

Dear Friend:
I request the pleasure of your company to accompany me to church on Sunday eve, June 3. One request I would like to make which, I presume, you will appreciate. As I have learned, your Father has gone out to Cherokee, which is not very far from Lamont, where my uncle, Doctor Hildenbrand, lives. He is considered a very prominent doctor. And if you will please give me your Father's address, [my uncle] should be glad to write to Him and give him a recommendation for me. I am sure he would give your Father a cordial welcome. Please answer as soon as convenient.
Yours sincerely,
Fred Schild

A written invitation, two weeks in advance, to walk to church, with references provided!

Although both sets of grandparents lived on farms, I was not isolated from other people on the one in Maryland. I found that I could walk almost anywhere I wanted to go—the one-room post office, the firehouse, a small grocery, the neighbors' house, or the church where my grandfather was pastor. For the first time in my life, I had a town I could encompass on foot, roads I could connect, faces that attached themselves to names I heard mentioned frequently over the supper table.

My grandmother, the neighborhood midwife, knew almost everyone in Marbury, and claimed to have delivered most of its children. On Sundays she would pile us all in the car early and go traveling about the back roads of Charles County with a trunk full of donated clothes. At every home along her circuit, she would stop and see if the children were ready for Sunday School. If they were, they would climb aboard. If the excuse was no clothes to wear, Mammaw would simply open the trunk, find something the right size, and another child would be crammed in the backseat.

I never once thought of Maryland as my home, any more than I thought of all the other places we had lived as home but, quite without knowing it, I was soaking up the setting for future books. When I grew up and settled in Bethesda, Maryland, I went back occasionally to Marbury—sometimes just to visit, then to bury Pappaw, and finally to bury

Mammaw. It wasn't until years later, on another nostalgic drive back, that I decided to place my next book there, a novel for adults called *Revelations*.

By the time I had placed a second novel, *A String of Chances*, in Marbury, and then a third, *Unexpected Pleasures*, I realized that this small southern Maryland town had worked its way into my blood. Driving along its one-lane roads, canopied with trees that opened up occasionally for a tobacco field, then closed again, past signs saying TURKEY SHOOT, EVERY SUNDAY, ELEVEN TILL THREE or JESUS SAVES AND HEALS, I could hear my grandparents' southern voices, the drawl of the hired man, the gossip, the complaints, the blessings.

If you rode through Marbury with me, you would see small boxlike houses on large hilly lots, signs saying FRESH BROWN EGGS or CHAIN-SAWS SHARPENED there on the front lawns. You would see the small cemetery where my grandparents were buried, an Exxon station, and sometimes three or four cars rusting in a side yard, but nothing that would distinguish this small town from hundreds of other rural communities across the country.

You would see a huge beech tree with my

cousins' initials carved in the trunk and a broken-down two-seater swing beneath it. But I would see my grandmother seated in that swing, holding court, impatiently ordering about the hired help. She would be thanking neighbors for the watermelons or the flowers or the sweet corn that people seemed incessantly to bring her for services rendered—babies birthed, wounds dressed, and advice given. You might see, on one of the back roads, a dilapidated house, overgrown with weeds, but I would see that porch teeming with children—so many, in fact, that the parents gave one of them to Pappaw and Mammaw to raise, and that little girl became my aunt.

Against the clipped Midwestern talk of my *maternal* grandparents, the southern accents of my paternal relatives oozed under my skin. The soft-spoken, chivalrous tones that my father used whenever he spoke to a woman; the little turns of phrase, such as "I might could get you some lemonade." Where my maternal grandparents would have said, "Phyllis, I won't put up with that nonsense another minute," my southern relatives would have told me, "I don't desire to suffer any more of your aggravation." These two sets of grandparents—these two very different

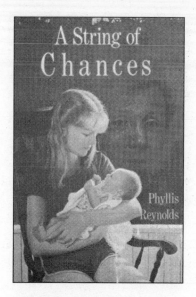

The jackets for *A String of Chances*, illustration by Ruth Sanderson, and *Send No Blessings*, illustration by Mary O' Keefe Young.

worlds—became the opposite poles of my life.

And because I've been married to a West Virginian longer than I ever remained under my parents' roof, I have come to love that state as well, and many of my novels, such as *Send No Blessings,* take place in Appalachia.

With the understanding of who I was and who my people were, there necessarily came reconciliation. As a young woman, I felt that one of the most damaging things my mother had done to me was to pass along her eternal worry, What will people think? What would the neighbors think if they saw me kissing a boyfriend on the front porch? What would the minister think if we were late to church? What would the teacher think if my ears were dirty?

Whatever else it did to me, however, it taught me to observe, to listen. Being sensitive to what one's characters are thinking and feeling is the first requisite of a writer, and if Mother's worry robbed me in one area, it enriched me in another.

I'm not happy unless I spend some time every day writing—even *thinking* about my writing will do. It's as though pressure builds up inside of me, and putting words on paper helps to release it. I jokingly tell my family that were I ever sentenced to solitary confinement, I would love it. I wouldn't, of course, but five or six hours a day of it would suit me fine.

For me, the very best part about writing is the point at which a character comes alive on paper, or when a place that existed only in my head becomes real. There are no bands playing, no audience applauding—a very private moment, actually—but it's an indescribable high.

The next best thing about writing is that I can be so many different characters in my books. In *A String of Chances*, I know what it is like to be Evie Hutchins with all her questions about God, and in the funeral scene, I cried along with her. In *The Solomon System*, I'm Ted, helping my older brother parallel park, or riding on the freeway beside him, my heart in my mouth. When Ellen April is alone in her mountain cabin in *Night Cry* and the dog begins to growl, I can feel the hair rising on the back of my own neck, and in *Send No Blessings,* when Beth Herndon discovers that her mother is expecting still another baby that Beth will have to care for, I suffer along with her.

Perhaps the drive to write, apart from the joy, comes from the realization that—although I can change my name, my vocation, my address, my *husband* even—I cannot, even for an instant, get outside my own body except in my imagination. I cannot physically ever experience what it is to be someone else. We are all prisoners forever inside our own skins. Writing, for me, is the way out—the way to "see what it would be like" to be someone else.

I used to love to act in plays, to paint with oils, and sing with a madrigal group, but I have given them all up to allow more time for writing. Sometimes, when I have a great deal of writing to do and very little time, I think it would be nice to live in one of those writing colonies where you have your own cottage, and lunch is placed on your doorstep every day. No meals to cook, no cats to feed, no phone. . . . But what would I write about? My family has appeared in my books in so many disguises that I would be lost without them. It's wonderful to get away for a while, but I need the stability of my home and friends to come back to after my imagination has carried me off. And so I go on living a life that is half in and half outside my head, and I can't think of anything I would like better.

I refuse to go on vacations until the first

draft of whatever book I'm working on is done, and then I leave it on my desk with all sorts of notes attached so that if I should drown in the ocean, my grieving relatives will know how I intended to revise it. I'm always worried that I might die too soon and that a whole family of characters will be trapped forever inside me. No one will ever know them. It's like a family going down in a boat at sea. So I write to give them a home and a place in a story.

When I'm working on a book, it is *always* on my mind. I go out for dinner with friends and to the theater with my husband, and we swim in the summer and hike in the fall, but the book is still with me. All the time. Everything I see, everything I do, is fuel somehow for the forming plot. When a story's going well I begin waking early in the mornings, hoping that it's time to get up so I can get on with it again. I seem to be constantly yanking myself back to the present time, forcing myself to concentrate on the moment, while another part of me is propelling itself into the future, into the next book and the next. Five years hence, I want to be able to pick up every book I have ever written and see how it could be improved—to know that if I were writing that book now, I would do it better.